An
Ancient
Future
Prayer

An Ancient Future Prayer

Uncover an Ancient Prayer that
Encompasses Your Entire Life

By Mike Greenberg

Windfarm Books
A DIV. OF DAILY AUDIO BIBLE

Dedication

To my family ~ Jennifer, I love you...thanks for your patience.
My kids, Ethan, Sarah & Aidan...be good & don't fight with each other!
I love you.

To all who have supported our family with prayers and finances.
You are an integral part of our lives and have helped with
bringing this book into existence.

And to the African front-liners who have allowed me to work with and walk with them,
throughout the continent. We love you and hope to see you soon.

ABOUT THE AUTHOR:

Mike & Jennifer recently celebrated 19 years of marriage; they have 3 children and live in Franklin, TN. After a year serving in Africa they have three major ministry focuses: The Word, Prayer & Missions. Discover what they do and how you can get involved at: www.HearAndTell.com

Acknowledgments:

Kyle Duncan & Geneva Atchison for your editorial expertise!
Thanks for allowing the Miguel Sanchisimo voice to come through.

Philip Karlan for all your design.
From the cover to the guts, you have been with me... year.

PREFACE:

What is. How to. To become.

This concept alone is 'worth the price of admission. I (Mike) can say that with confidence, as the concept does not originate with me; I learned it from two very smart men in South Africa who have made an immeasurable impact on my life. So please allow me to honor John Smith and Hennie Hanekom. I met John and Hennie when my family and I spent a year living and working in South Africa in 2010.

Let's take a moment to look at this three-part phrase, "what is, how to, to become." These three short thoughts are powerfully connected. As we examine them, picture their role like setting the lighting before a play. Establishing the mood and what is highlighted.

Here's how it works:

What is…
What is a soccer player? It's a person who plays soccer!

How to…
How do you play soccer? There are two teams, and two goals; each team tries to kick the soccer ball into the goal.

To become…
After you practice and learn how to play, it becomes natural and a part of you—and you "become a soccer player."

Another example:

What is…
What is a nurse? A nurse is someone who helps doctors with their patients.

How to…
How do you become a nurse? You go to nursing school, you
intern, you train and learn how to become a nurse.

To become…
Finally after some time, your nursing skills become part of who you
are, how you respond to situations and you **become** a nurse.

To explain the idea of what is, how to, and to become is to first
of all, offer a new way of viewing various roles in your life, or the lives
of friends and family. You can see friends who want "to become" something but they are still in the "how to" phase, or maybe even the "what
is" phase. Last example, I promise. My daughter is learning how to
play percussion instruments. She is in both the what is, and the how to
phase and perhaps if she sticks with it she'll become a percussionist.

With this Ancient Future Prayer, the hope is not to waste
words, but to quickly explain the "what is…" of this prayer.

Then, offer a few examples regarding the "how to," specifically
"how *I* do" this Ancient Future Prayer, and to provide enough ideas and examples for each section of the prayer, so that you can then make it your own.

After you get the pattern, then on a regular basis begin
to fill in the prayer with what's happening in your life… that this
prayer **"becomes"** part of who you are. It's a simple concept,
so let's dive in to the what is, some of the how to, so that this
prayer concept becomes natural… daily laying a holistic pattern
where you connect and converse with your Creator.

Overarching Concepts

Ancient Future: Preserving or adding ancient aspects to
modern elements. Taking modern settings and adding
ancient elements. Giving new life to old traditions.

An example of Ancient Future worship. Some churches have
tossed out ancient traditions because they can become stale, boring and
seemingly irrelevant. So you could walk into some churches today and have
no idea you are in a church. Coffee is flowing, a band is kicking out a funky
version of "Jesus Loves Me This I Know," and the person at the front tells
better jokes than most stand-up comedians. And none of those things are
inherently wrong. Then you walk into a church that has held on to certain
ancient traditions like burning incense or reading together out-loud prayers,
where the person up front has on a very interesting robe. A focus of an ancient/
future worship service would assimilate elements of the past along with
elements of today, and a good blend moves us into a potentially rich future.

This book is not titled *Ancient Future Prayer,*
because what it is not is a book about ancient/future praying.

This book is not called *The Ancient Future Prayer*, because that doesn't exist.

It's called **An Ancient Future Prayer** because it takes an
ancient prayer, or model of prayer (about 2,000 years old), and
mixes it, or overlays it, on top of who/where we are, living and
breathing today. It actually doesn't lie on top, but more lies underneath,
to form a base. But it doesn't matter if you see it lying on top or
underneath; it's like the question of chicken and the
egg… best answer is just enjoy the meal.
This ancient prayer is something that we can place our
whole self (*the three-layered man) on top of.

Disclaimer: When the word Man is said in this book in terms like, "the three-layered man," it simply means the same as person or humankind. Not just men. A shout out to all the ladies in the house! You're awesome.

*What's the three-layered man? The three-layered man is, all of us... what we are made out of, what we are made up of. And if we are going to look at our lives entirely, holistically, and healthily, then we need to look at all three layers: *Physical, Spiritual & Emotional.*

Thus I offer to you... **An Ancient Future Prayer**:
The Ancient Prayer that has been named "The Lord's Prayer," overlaid with Today's Three-Layered Man. I pray you discover a Majestic Mosaic. One that shapes the way you live, pray and affect those around you.

Prayer Preface

How long have people been praying? What is prayer? Do we pray every day? Religiously, repetitively, from the heart? To whom do we pray?

"Prayers are the seeds that germinate within our soul, sprout faith and produce life-giving fruit. Fruit such as direction, clarification, wisdom, guidance, comfort and so much more." -Brian Hardin

Some prayers we've memorized and they've lost the "heart meaning" in our daily lives. The ancient prayer that we will look at is a couple thousand years old, and has relevance in every area of our lives every day.

Many of us can rattle off this prayer in a matter of seconds, and walk right past all that it has for us. Gifts that are available to us like relieving stress, the freedom of forgiving others, gaining comfort, and direction in the day and age we live in.

Let's look at this ancient prayer as a model, a structure; like the bones of a body. Without the bone structure you have no shape or form. And without the organs, blood, muscle and tissue around the bone structure, you have no life.

I have three things in the morning (actually four); when these things happen, I feel much better about my day and my life. That is: 1. Some sort of exercise, 2. Listening to the Daily Audio Bible Podcast, 3. Praying through this ancient prayer (about a 30 - minute time), and the 4th item goes without saying - because really it doesn't matter if I exercise, pray or take my spiritual Bible vitamins, I will have a cup of coffee… interesting to see what takes precedent. Coffee 1st - definitely some time in emails throughout the day, a little Facebook, some TV, most likely breakfast, lunch and dinner, and work. But if I do those 3 things in the morning-Exercise, Pray & Bible - then life is good, and direction is well set. **However, they are the first things to go out the window, and many times they do.**

How do we get our lives on course? How do we get off the merry-go-round and really walk daily in the higher purposes that we have? We are created for much more than working tirelessly to achieve the "American dream."

As we work through the simple principles that I've been praying through personally for years, we will discover a model that daily touches on everything in our entire lives.

I offer to you what I believe will help center your focus and give you insight into what the Creator of the universe would have in store for you.

I'm not a scientist, theologian or psychologist, but I've heard it said enough, that I believe we would all agree that as humans, we are made up of three separate, distinct attributes that are woven together to form who we are:

1. The physical
2. The emotional
3. The spiritual

Which one of these attributes of a human is most important? The physical? As some would say, "If you stop smoking, exercise, eat organically, floss your teeth, and look a certain way, you will be happy, healthy and people will like you." But emotionally, you're depressed, isolated and lonely.

Or is the emotional part the most important? You never get stressed, you have peace amidst the storm, you are a loving person, but it all ends there. Spiritually, you have no growth within you.

Or is the spiritual piece the most important? If you pray and read your Bible every day you'll be a strong little soldier in God's army, but you eat poorly, don't take care of yourself, and you're falling apart physically, and you could make choices that would change that.

If one of these three parts is out of balance, it's all out of balance. You and I must be holistically healthy.

If that phrase raises red flags in your head, let's dig into this together. If we lean on spiritual first, it shapes the emotional… but I think where most people who profess Christ lose respect by their neighbors and the nations is we stop short and don't execute our lives like everything and all matter. But let's discuss this as we move on together.

The ancient prayer we are about to explore covers all areas of our lives (physical, spiritual and emotional), setting your focus as you enter your day in a right direction.

When Jesus was asked by His followers, "Teach us how to pray," shouldn't we be arrested by His answer? Or should we just move along and "make it up as we go?"

It doesn't matter who you are, or whether you believe Jesus is someone who should be listened to, when His followers ask it as plainly as this, "teach us how to pray." His answer is short, to the point, and amazingly full of life. His answer is something we might want to examine, receive and perhaps… give a deeper look to. Sadly most simply memorize it as a child and walk on. Let's walk in.

And Jesus answered and said:

OUR FATHER IN HEAVEN,

HALLOWED BE YOUR NAME.

YOUR KINGDOM COME.

YOUR WILL BE DONE

ON EARTH AS IT IS IN HEAVEN.

GIVE US THIS DAY OUR DAILY BREAD.

AND FORGIVE US OUR DEBTS,

AS WE FORGIVE OUR DEBTORS.

AND DO NOT LEAD US INTO TEMPTATION,

BUT DELIVER US FROM THE EVIL ONE.

FOR YOURS IS THE KINGDOM AND THE

POWER AND THE GLORY FOREVER. AMEN.

As we look at *some of the aspects of this prayer, you
will find yourself touched in every part of your life, and
the lives of people that can be affecting you.

*This is my disclaimer… anyone claiming to have exhausted what
has been called, "The Lord's Prayer," is most likely short sighted.

What we will walk through together is a model within The Model. The model is what Jesus gave us. However, I believe and have found that as a model, a structure, a foundation to walk through even daily, it is not something that can be memorized. It is not something that can be written down—it is something that changes all the time, with the winds of our lives and as we pray through it.

What we have is a foundation laid that gives us so much life and wisdom and direction that it cannot be exhausted.

So let's go.

Our Father In Heaven
Hallowed Be Thy Name!

Always begin with worship. Sometimes this is the most difficult thing to do. When you are depressed or sad, when you are going through a hard time, or when you just stayed up too late and you're tired. Be thankful. Be grateful to our Creator. He is Almighty.

Complaining leads to negative health issues. Looking at the glass half empty is not as fun or fulfilling as looking at it half full. There's a thing called a "Thank offering." And I tried it today. I was feeling a little confused and down about a few things, but just started saying "thank You" to God about all kinds of stuff. The more I did it, the happier I became, and the more things I found I could be thankful for.

When the bills are piling up and you don't know how they are going to get paid… what can you be thankful for? One thing I said thanks about was realizing I have never missed a meal, slept on dirt floors, or had the rain coming down on me or my family as we slept at night. When all around seems in despair, find something to be thankful for.

One thing about me is… I have A.D.D. tendencies. I'm easily distracted like the dog in the movie *Up!* ("Squirrel!") So, one thing that has helped me over the years is to walk outside when I pray. This practice makes it difficult when you travel in certain situations and in different weather conditions. But, my point is, I've heard about these people who wake up at four in the morning and pray by their bedside by candlelight… I'd be back to sleep in no time flat. It just doesn't work for me! Does that mean I'm lazy and undisciplined? Maybe. But, does it mean, "that" is the only righteous and right way to pray? I don't think so. And I certainly hope not.

For years I've felt guilty about my spiritual disciplines and the lack thereof, hearing over and over the story of one saint who positioned himself in the bathtub with his head against the wall while he prayed. This way if he fell asleep he would slip and hit his head on the water spigot—this would obviously keep him alert

and awake to keep praying in the early mornings! WHAT?!
Is that really what sainthood prayers are about? If it is… I'm in trouble.

I had this underlying guilt of never praying enough—oh yeah, and also the fact that I could use more exercise from working behind a computer every day! So praying and walking made sense, and I love to do it!

I started near our neighborhood in Ventura, California where, thankfully, in such a busy city we had a walk path that was serene with a lot of trees near our house.

I remember many times just walking and looking up through the leaves into the sky, seeing the clouds and worshiping the Creator. Telling Him how thankful I was for His intricately creating the world. The leaves that helped with the oxygen I breathe. The colors and diversity in the trees. This is ONE example of worship, within the first parts of our praying.

In your times of thanksgiving you can begin to introduce the concept of the three-layered man here, like this.

Spiritually, what can you be thankful for?
Example. "I'm thankful that I have a Bible. I'm thankful for certain books or friends who encourage me spiritually. I'm thankful for the nature that surrounds me, that screams at my spirit what a great God and creator You are."

Physically, what can you be appreciative of?
Example: "Thank you God for my health, my kids' health. Thank you God for food, air, etc." Physically what can you begin to give thanks for?

Emotionally, what can we thank God for? Example: "Thank you God for peace; amidst the craziness of life, You offer peace."

As we move on, we will unpack the idea of the three-layered man more.

An Ancient Future Prayer is not a study on the Names of God. There are many great resources available. Even a quick google search took me to the Blue Letter Bible and a list of several of the names of God and what they mean, like:

Jehovah-Raah: The Lord My Shepherd
How do we need, or want God to
shepherd our life? Worship and thank Him.

"Our Father, who is in Heaven," and we
say to Him, "Hallowed be Thy name."

Jehovah Jireh: The Lord Will Provide
Thank Him that He knows what we need, and He will provide...
we will look more closely at provision in the coming sections.

What does Hallowed mean?
To honor as holy, set aside to be worshipped, adored and praised. And then you begin to look at some of the other names and attributes of God:

Creator. A great start is to start at the start: God made this place. Get outside the mall or coffee shop and take a look around—God's handiwork is amazing! The more you look, the more you will worship our Father who is in heaven and understand that His name is worthy of praise and adoration. One of His names or major aspects is... Creator.

Alpha and Omega. Worship He who is the
beginning and the end. And the One "who has begun a good
work in you will carry it to completion." —Philippians 1:6

El Shaddai. He is "God all Sufficient."

Do a quick search online for many of the beautiful names of God, so you can begin to worship aspects of Him. When you speak the words "Hallowed be Thy name," you can linger and experience and express worship to "Our Father who is in heaven" and worship aspects of Him you may not have thought to worship, like:

Jehovah-Shalom: "The Lord our Peace," as He is referred to in Judges 6:24.

You could spend 30 minutes within the first two lines: Our Father in Heaven, hallowed be thy Name.

And some days you may get caught up in worshipping and not move on to these next sections. And that's ok, this model prayer is the bone structure, and what you may need to spend time on today could look totally different tomorrow.

Worship Him—tell Him how great He is and how grateful you are. He is worthy of praise and thanks.

Let the worship of our Creator cleanse some of the worthless things weighing you down.

OUR FATHER IN HEAVEN ~ HALLOWED BE THY NAME!
::: Section Reflection :::

What are a few things you can write down that you are thankful for?

_____

_____

_____

_____

_____

_____

_____

_____

_____

_____

_____

_____

_____

YOUR KINGDOM COME

There is nothing like His Kingdom! There is no better way than His. He is all knowing. He sees all. We see parts, at best.

When we say… "Thy Kingdom Come," what are we saying? We rush right past it. We repeat it over and over throughout our lives, but… what are we asking for when we say, "Thy Kingdom Come?"

One day I felt the question come up, like this, "Tell me about My Kingdom." If God asked you this, what would be your answer? Take a moment. Answer. If God asked you a very, very simple question —"Tell me about My kingdom"— what would you say?

I want to know what you would say your thoughts on 'the Kingdom.'

I was arrested with the thought: "Mike, you say to Me all the time, 'Thy Kingdom Come.' Why? What do you mean, Mike? What is it you are asking for?"

As I'm walking and praying, I might notice that the roads are paved with dirt rock and tar. I say to Him, "I've read about your Kingdom in Heaven—the streets are apparently paved with gold. What we consider as having MUCH value is used to pave the roads in Your Kingdom. A lot of people are collecting and selling gold, and your streets are made if it?!" Wow! Awesome Kingdom. But it's WAY more than gold-paved streets.

I've heard that there are no tears or crying in heaven. Apparently, everyone is happy, giving thanks and saying 'Holy, Holy, Holy is the Lord God Almighty.' It is also written in the Bible about the peace You bring, not like the peace the world gives, but Your peace that You give.

So, all that sounds like the 'sweet by and by' in the afterlife, like a fairytale. But… Jesus taught us to pray saying, "Thy kingdom come ON EARTH as it is in heaven."

One thing I know about an earthly kingdom, is what the king says goes. And if the king is a good king, what he says is for the good of the people in the kingdom.

Apparently in Your kingdom there is no hunger; there are a lot of hungry people in the world. Apparently in Your Kingdom there are many mansions, and if there weren't many mansions, Jesus would have told us that… well there are a lot of homeless people in the world. In Your Kingdom You reign there; it seems like the rich rule here where we live. What You say goes in Your Kingdom! Your way IS the Highway—and there is no other way but Your way.

Again to remind us… this is a model going through The Model ancient prayer. What we just went over is an example, of when we are praying, "Thy Kingdom Come," of aspects of His Kingdom we are saying 'come.' We are praying for His Kingdom, His Life, His provision, His Reign, His Peace, His Healing, His ways to "be done."

"On earth as it is in Heaven." For me… it seemed a little "big" to be praying for the whole earth at one time. So as I thought through what I was praying—"Thy Kingdom come on EARTH"—I was able to think and pray through what in the world do I mean when I say "on earth?" Am I tossing out a hopeful thought for all mankind? Like, "God bless everyone." Is that effective? If we were to just say over and over, "God bless the whole world, God bless the whole world, God bless the whole world," would God finally throw up His hands and say… "OK! I'll bless the whole world!" What are we saying when we say, "Thy Kingdom come, Thy will be done on earth as it is in heaven?"

Well, if we aren't praying for the whole world at one time, are we at least praying for our nation, or our city, or our neighborhood? Could we pray, "Thy Kingdom come, Thy will be done in my neighborhood, just like it is in heaven...?"

I think we can pray for the world...I think we can pray for our nation, and we certainly should be praying for our nation's leaders.

I love prayer walking through my neighborhood praying blessings on and over my neighbors, and there are some strong scriptures about doing that.

But for me to BOIL IT ALL DOWN, WHAT does it mean when I say the words, "Thy Kingdom come, Thy will be done, on earth as it is in heaven"? For me... It's this:

How does THAT look in MY life, in me and then through me?!

That (in my opinion) is HUGE! Let's walk through it: Thy Kingdom Come—in me as YOU see it. So if we have answered God, "what do you mean when you say, 'Thy Kingdom come?' and He says, "Tell me about My Kingdom," and let's say we just PICK ONE ASPECT, and it's PEACE, and we say, "Thy Kingdom come (and in your Kingdom is Peace that passes all understanding) in me as it is in heaven."

Here's what it would sound like... "Let Your Peace come in me as it is in heaven." Say it again and think about that for a second, "let Your Peace come in me as it is in heaven."

If you're at all like me it begins to feel like: "ahhh, that tastes, (and sounds) pretty good; can we pick another one and do it again?"

Luke 17:20: Now when He was asked by the Pharisees when the kingdom of God would come, He answered them and said, "The kingdom of God does not come with observation; nor will they say, 'See here!' or 'See there!' For indeed, the kingdom of God is within you."

Let it start today in the mirror. With you, in you, and through you.

OK—another aspect of His Kingdom is provision.

"Thy Kingdom come on earth as it is in heaven" normally sounds like, "God bless America… amen," when it CAN SOUND LIKE:

"May your perfect provision come in me as You would have it be." And the way that He would have it be is fulfilling all of His great ideas that He has for You—which is far better than what we would even have for ourselves. And the way that it not only affects you directly, but the way that it flows to and through you touching others, is His good and perfect will!

Talk to God about His Kingdom; research what some of His names mean. Worship Him for some of the aspects of who He is that are revealed to you, like Savior, Healer, Provider, Father, Giver of life, Lover of justice… Tell Him about His Kingdom and ask Him to reveal aspects of His Kingdom to you, and ask Him when you pray, that aspects of His Kingdom would come in your life today… in you and through you.

YOUR KINGDOM COME
::: Section Reflection :::

When you say "Thy kingdom come" right now, in your
personal life, what element of His kingdom would you ask for?

_____

_____

_____

_____

_____

_____

_____

_____

_____

_____

_____

THY WILL BE DONE

You may have a good idea of what you'd like to see done, but...
God truly knows best. There is no better way than His way. There
is no better will than His will. He has your best interests in mind.
He loves you. He wants to see you free and living the life He
created you to live. But most of the time we have a direction that we
want to go in... so we go in that direction and ask God to go with us.
Thankfully, He is very patient and loving with us, but... giving up
control, and not asking Him to tag along with your ideas, but to have
Him actually lead, brings the most freedom and the fullest life available.

Many times we will do this for years and years, digging a
rutted path that can only take a major event to disrupt the
pattern. Sometimes it's a miracle, sometimes it's a mid-life crisis,
sometimes it's a death, or a revelation where we say, "Something has
got to change, and change drastically, or I'm going to lose it! I'm
dissatisfied with my job, my life, and my existence. The time I have with
my family is less than quality... how in the world did I end up here?"

Most likely, by choice—your choice, and asking God to bless
your choices, as opposed to following Him, jumping into the cavernous
future that involves faith and trust but ends up in fruit-filled treasure.

The sooner we move forward in life following Him and not
asking Him to follow and bless us, the better! I believe the answer lies
within this ancient future prayer. All the sections that we go over
together are examples; they will vary from person to person and from
day to day, but the majestic mosaic that will be laid will become His!

Many times when someone is obedient to what they believe God
is saying (i.e. feel in their heart... "say no to this," or "say yes to this")
the natural response or the educated response can be, "That's crazy, and
totally counter to the culture I live in!" What do you mean turn down
this promotion? Or, what do you mean, "follow Me here, or go over

there?" Sometimes it's only after getting down the path a ways and looking back that you can see and realize… He knew more than you could have known on your own, and the best thing would have been to listen.

When you pray "Thy will be done," what are you praying or saying? Do you truly believe that He has your best interests in mind? Do you trust Him? Have you tried, and watched Him guide and provide? If not, it's high time you step out and trust, and see the hand of God alive and well in your life.

Is everything in your life manufactured, concocted, and contain a "Plan B"?

Thy will be done…what are you facing in your life? What decision? What issue, what item can you lay in His hands and say, "Not my will but Thy will be done."

Many times we say we are followers of God or Jesus, when the reality is, we believe in God and Jesus, and we try to follow some of the precepts taught in the Bible, but we are not truly following His will for our lives. We chart out our lives and we ask God to come along and bless it. When you pray, "Thy will be done," what do you hear Him whisper in your heart? What leap of faith might He be calling you to take?

We spend a lot getting advice from other sources when the God who made it all, and knows it all, is also called "our wonderful counselor," and wants to freely give us direction and wisdom.

The provision and direction may not be what you had in mind, but give it over to Him and don't move off of ~ four words that can shape your tomorrow.

"Thy will be done."

THY WILL BE DONE
::: *Section Reflection* :::

What can you write down that you are facing at this
time in your life… a direction that you want God's will
to be done in? Write it down. Pray and trust.

Give Us This Day Our Daily Bread :
PHYSICALLY

When we memorize a prayer like The Lord's Prayer, and it becomes mechanical and rote, we can run right past aspects as we grab our morning coffee and race into our day after, day after daze.

I've asked several people what they think it means for God to "give us our daily bread," and have heard a few answers. One is, "Jesus is our daily bread." He said, "I am the Bread of Life. Take and eat of me." When we receive the communion elements of the bread and wine, some believe that this is done in 'remembrance' of what Jesus did for us on the cross, while others believe that it is the actual body and blood of our Savior. I'm not throwing my hat in the ring with any of the arguments on this, but want to give you my perspective on a daily level perspective, how when I pray through this model prayer that Jesus gave us, when I reach the point of, "Give us this day our daily bread," how I see and pray through it.

God is good, and God is great, and I again want to emphasize that I'm not taking anything away from a doctrine of the daily bread, but…to add an angle or element that has really, really helped me.

First and foremost, it's this: God does not need a reminder to feed me today!

Think about it for a second…have you ever prayed, "And give us this day our daily bread" with the fleeting thought pro-cess of, "By the way God, please don't forget to feed me today"?

The way Jesus answered, and the prayer model He gave… works always and everywhere! Much of my heart is in Africa. Where daily bread for many, is just that… "daily bread." This book was not created to be a dogmatic how to, and how not to pray. Nor a discussion on global justice or injustice… and why I was born where I was born and when I was born ~ the point at hand is, as in all things, whatever we consider big or small we are to look to Him for provision.

If you are looking for books on global justice and how to get involved, I'd highly suggest *The Hole in Our Gospel*, by Richard Stearns of World Vision.

Well, let's go back to what's the most important aspect of our human condition… is it spiritual, physical or emotional? It's holistic. It's encompassing. There are verses that talk about caring for the whole person. Like in Matthew 25. And in Luke 2:52 describing how Jesus grew.

Matthew 10:28 says, "do not be afraid of those who kill the body but cannot kill the soul. Rather, be afraid of the One who can destroy both soul and body in hell."

This book's goal & purpose is to grow spiritually in PRAYER, connected to the Creator, relinquishing our will and learning of and leaning into His purposes for our lives, which will touch us on a physical, emotional and certainly a spiritual level.

What I don't want this to endorse is a departure of responsibility that WE HAVE on the physical.

So hopefully this doesn't digress into a ridiculous conversation. But one that makes us aware that not only is God interested in all of who we are, physically, emotionally and spiritually… but we also have a responsibility in all of those areas.

I believe that Philippians 4:19 is true: "And my God will meet all your needs according to his glorious riches in Christ Jesus."

The question is… what do you need?

My answer, for me, is… I need to do His will. Jesus said in John 4, "I have food that you know not of… My food, is to do the will of Him who sent me…"

We just finished praying through… "Thy Kingdom come… THY will be done…on earth as it is in heaven…" Your Kingdom come, Your reign in me, Your will be done in me as You would have it be!

So what would His daily bread accomplish in my life if He provided it? I think it would accomplish His will which for all people starts at the cross of Christ. When we confess with our mouth and believe with our hearts that Jesus came to earth, lived a sinless life, died on the cross and rose from the dead—for the forgiveness of our sins and to give us new life… then we are clean, forgiven, and ready to take new and next steps in following God's ideas for our lives. That's the foundation.

Here is how I work through "give us this day our daily bread." I'll mix it up on what I pray through first… sometimes I'll pray through the physical aspects first.

Example: "Lord, give me this day, everything I need in order to do Your will today physically." Items in the physical include finances, transportation, lodging, food, physical strength — anything physical.

Now remember… this is not a reminder for God to not forget to feed you. And if God truly cares about every aspect of our lives, it's not a reminder to Him about ANYTHING!

Matthew 6:7-8: "And when you pray, do not keep on babbling like pagans, for they think they will be heard because of their many words. Do not be like them, for your Father knows what you need before you ask him."

He knows! This is not a reminder to the all-knowing Creator that you may need a ride to work today.

If it's a reminder at all… to whom is it a reminder?

To wrap up thoughts about the physical aspect of man in regard
to "give us this day our daily bread," a final example would be:

"Father, You are my provider, give me everything I need
today to do Your will physically. You know what my bank account looks
like, and You also know what my needs are; You are concerned with my
whole life's story, not just getting me through this day. So I believe
and trust in You for what is before me. And I believe that physically,
You can provide whatever is needed for me to walk in Your will for my life."

It's such a simple and freeing phrase for me now... "Give us this
day our daily bread." To borrow a phrase from U2's lead singer Bono:
"What you don't have, you don't need it now." If you are desiring
to do the will of the Father, and it is His good and perfect will to
provide you everything you need to fulfill that, He will provide for
you this day everything you need physically to do His will... this
simplifies everything. If we can rest in and trust our Father.

He cares, His will is best, even if it doesn't "make sense." If I'm
relinquishing myself to follow Him... He will
provide what I need to do His will!

GIVE US THIS DAY OUR DAILY BREAD : PHYSICALLY
::: *Section Reflection* :::

What do you need provided by God today physically that would assist in you walking in His will and ways for your life?

_____

_____

_____

_____

_____

_____

_____

_____

_____

_____

_____

GIVE US THIS DAY
OUR DAILY BREAD :
SPIRITUALLY
GIVE TO ME THIS DAY, WHAT I NEED SPIRITUALLY TO DO YOUR WILL
TODAY, NOT ONLY IN MY LIFE BUT ALSO THOSE IN MY INFLUENCE

Here's where it "seems a little easier." Because God is Spirit and those who worship Him must worship Him in spirit and truth. His worshippers are truly desirous and trust Him that His will is the best for their lives. "Your will be done, not mine, because I trust You, I've worshiped You (or aspects of You) and You are truly good... Please provide everything spiritually I need today to do Your will."

Well... of course God would do that. He has plenty of Bible verses to feed me spiritually today. In other words, He's certainly not short on ways He can feed me spiritually. So to ask God to give me everything I need today to do His will spiritually, could seem ridiculous.

But that's how we look at this section of the Lord's Prayer, without even considering it. We say, "give us this day our daily bread..." and we fail to remember we are made up of spirit, soul and body.

What do you need spiritually? Well... it's like what we need physically: most of us eat every day. Most of us don't just grab a snack once a week. Similarly, our spiritual "gas tank" determines our "emotional gas-tank." If we are spiritually full of the Good God stuff, the emotional result is Good God emotions and Good God physical works as well.

Which is the most important aspect of the human condition to focus on? Emotional, physical or spiritual? It seems like we shouldn't leave any area behind. We must exercise (feed) them all! Physical exercise generally makes people feel better emotionally, and can sometimes play a role in how we treat others. When we feel physically well, it tends to be easier to emotionally treat others well.

Also, first for something to flow through us, it must flow to us. So, if we are spiritually able to pour into the lives of those around us, we need to be mindful in asking God to provide for us this, day, what we need spiritually to do His will, in and through us.

What do we need spiritually to do the will of God for our lives? Is this something that we get or gain from Sunday morning at church? Do we get or gain that from personal reading? Reading what? What is the healthiest for you spiritually to absorb, and how much?

Here's maybe even a better question: What do we need spiritually in our lives today to serve others the way God wants for us to serve them?

What if your time spent in prayer resulted in you encouraging someone during the day that needed the encouragement. What if your time reading the Bible made a scripture stand out and it was "just what someone needed to hear from you today?"

Ask God to provide and direct you in the best path to receive spiritually what you need to do His will. He provides in many ways.

Some of the ways we receive spiritually from God: through other people, while in prayer, by reading or meditating on His Word, the Bible, or through our surroundings (i.e. sometimes if we are listening we can grow spiritually by paying attention to the world that God created and placed us in).

As you ask God to give you what you need spiritually to do His will today, be conscious of some of the various ways He may deliver them to you. He is creative! Then see what He's given you that might be helpful to someone He brings across your path, or someone you regularly interact with.

Spiritually
Give us this day our daily bread
Give to me this day what I need spiritually to do Your will today, not only in my life but also those in my influence.

GIVE US THIS DAY OUR DAILY BREAD : SPIRITUALLY
::: *Section Reflection* :::

What are some ways that God has provided for you
spiritually that you may have disregarded?

_____

_____

_____

_____

_____

_____

_____

_____

_____

_____

_____

_____

_____

_____

GIVE US THIS DAY
OUR DAILY BREAD :
EMOTIONALLY

Many times the emotional aspect is the part I personally wrestle through the most.

Another note/reminder: In every aspect, none of what is offered is exhaustive, none of it... So if I leave off an example of a specific emotion that may be a big part of your life, just insert the thought or emotion in the reading.

First let's look at a few emotions and a few of their opposites. There are many lists of emotions, but one baseline focus I like to use is found in the Bible in Galatians 5:22-23; and it is interesting that the names of these emotions are called the fruit (or result of) the Spirit ~ these nine emotional attributes are not called the Spirit, but the result (fruit) of the Spirit: "But the fruit of the Spirit is love, joy, peace, patience, kindness, goodness, faithfulness, gentleness and self-control."

Wow! If I could nail those attributes, I would be a different person! Just pick ONE of the nine mentioned. Let's look at a couple of them... starting with love.

GIVE US THIS DAY
OUR DAILY BREAD :
EMOTIONALLY : LOVE

Love. It's a simple thing to look at: who do we love, what do we love, how do we love? Love is the baseline of our Godly human existence.

In John Chapter 13:35 Jesus said: "By this all men will know that you are my disciples, if you love one another." Far too many times people who say they follow Jesus do not share, or show the true love of the Father… and that has a major impact on people's belief that God is, and that God loves. So the fruit of the Spirit is a collection of very important "emotions," and is a bottom line of what God wants to get to us and through us as a result of spiritual growth evidence.

We say that we love our spouses, our dogs, and ice-cream sandwiches. When something or someone "rubs us the wrong way," we "fall out of love" pretty easily. Is that the kind of love you need today? Is that the way you want to be loved? Thankfully, God loves us with less of a fickle love than we have for others.

When we receive physically, spiritually and emotionally it starts with us looking up, and seeing God exemplify it, and providing it; you receive it (appropriate it), and then you can give it. In steps, it looks like this:

First, there needs to be an acceptance of God's love for us. Second, there needs to be a love for ourselves, seeing us the way God sees us. If we hate everything about ourselves, we are obviously not seeing ourselves the way God sees us.

Here's another way of putting it. Let's call it *appropriating*.

First we appropriately experience an emotion that God has. Like peace. God has a lot of peace! We witness it in Jesus. God has a lot of patience and Love. We see it appropriately. We see it biblically. We experience it. We see and get a taste of it. That's the "looking up."

Then we internalize it, towards us. God loves me. God has patience
with me! God takes joy in me. You apply this in your life. You internalize this.
That's the "looking in."

Then we externalize it, towards others. I will have
patience with others. I will love others. I will love my neighbor.
That's the "looking out."

That entire three-part process, I call *appropriating*.
Seeing it properly, receiving it and giving or living it. And when
one of the elements breaks down, and we misappropriate what
God can and would supply for us to do His will… like,
exemplifying His patience with others, then we "blow it," sin or trespass.

Give us this day our daily bread (can sound like):
God, give me the love that I need today.
It's looking up and seeing the love God has for you.
(How does God see you?)
It's looking in and seeing yourself the way God loves you.
(How do you see you?)
It's looking out to see others with godly love. (How do you see others?)

Is love essential? Is it part of our lives once a week, or daily?
Give us this day our daily bread… the love
that we need today, to do Your will.

GIVE US THIS DAY
OUR DAILY BREAD :
EMOTIONALLY : JOY

Give me this day the joy I need to do Your will.

What situations are you facing? What is taking your joy away? What might you bump into today, that you would need some serious joy to handle?

Joy is not necessarily being happy or "giddy." Here's a definition of Joy: The emotion evoked by well-being, success, or good fortune or by the prospect of possessing what one desires.

I like how it says "the prospect." It's not the way the world works; however, we get joy when we GET the thing, not when we have the "prospect" of getting.

Here's a Bible verse about joy from the book of Philippians in chapter 4. "Rejoice in the Lord always; again I will say, Rejoice. Let your reasonableness be known to everyone. The Lord is at hand; do not be anxious about anything…"

God has joy for you - ask Him to provide the joy you need to do His will today. Imagine facing some of the daily things with a big 'ol bunch of God-given joy!

It will make a lot of the tedious melt away into history.

Ask Him for the joy you need today to do His will.

Give Us This Day
Our Daily Bread :
EMOTIONALLY : PEACE

Give me this day the peace I need to do Your will.

Read John 14:27: "Peace I leave with you; my peace
I give you. I do not give to you as the world gives. Do not
let your hearts be troubled and do not be afraid."

So… how does the world give peace?

What are some of the things that come to mind that
offer peace in the world? God comes to you and says… I've
got peace for you, but… you'll have to trust Me.

We (in post-modern western societies) don't normally reach
for peace. We lean towards 'escapism.' Burying our face in the
latest fiction novel, movie or TV series ~ and I am not against those
things in totality, but definitely many times when we could reach
for the peace God has for us, we short-cut through escapism.
If we really believe that there is a God, who loves us, and
really has the best life waiting for us if we trust and follow Him, then
why do we try to escape from reality so often? Why do I do that?!
We have a God who is very patient with us. Just consider the time
and money that we waste. He has been very patient with me.

Peace. His peace. That's really what we're looking for.
But we continue to seek out our peace from other sources.
Give me this day the peace I need today to do Your will.

GIVE US THIS DAY
OUR DAILY BREAD :
EMOTIONALLY :
PATIENCE, KINDNESS, GENTLENESS,
FAITHFULNESS, GOODNESS AND SELF-CONTROL

Go through each of the nine fruit of the spirit as you pray. Ask God to give you this day all the patience, you'll need today to do His will.

Pray for all the kindness you will need this day to do His will. All the gentleness.

Pray for faithfulness, goodness and self-control. Certain times in your life, aspects will be more prominent than in other times. You may be in a season where you really need a whole lot of self-control. Ask God to provide all the self-control you need this day to do His will.

Give us this day our daily bread. All the gentleness I need today, to do your will in and through my life.

*Those are some examples of emotions. When I go through the nine mentioned in the fruit of the spirit, it really seems to round out every aspect I'm dealing with, or most likely going to be dealing with that day… Unfortunately, I don't always, "appropriate" the gifts the Father is working to give me emotionally (like patience for example), and I seriously blow it in one way or another. Which leads very nicely into the next section… forgive me.

GIVE US THIS DAY OUR DAILY BREAD
EMOTIONALLY : LOVE, JOY, PEACE, PATIENCE, KINDNESS, GENTLENESS, FAITHFULNESS, GOODNESS AND SELF-CONTROL

::: *Section Reflection* :::

What are you needing provided to you this day emotionally?

_____

_____

_____

_____

_____

_____

_____

_____

_____

_____

_____

_____

_____

_____

_____

AND FORGIVE US OUR DEBTS

Wouldn't that be nice? Any debt. Any credit card bills, anything we owed… forgiven. The stuff that we've gotten ourselves into. The impulsive decisions we made without the counsel of prayer or other people. Gone.

Is that really a possibility? Or is it just talking about "sin." Like, ya know, killing somebody. Or getting mad at someone and cussing them out, ripping them apart verbally. That kind of stuff… God can forgive and make right. Or is there more available?

Another Bible version says, "Forgive us our trespasses." But what's a trespass? Where I come from that's when there is a sign on someone's property that says "no trespassing," and you "trespass" or walk where you should not be walking—which is the opposite of walking where you should be walking.

We can look at the etymology: debt, trespass and sin. But for simplicity's sake, let's use the word picture of someone trespassing on a piece of property that he/she should not be on, which means that person is not walking where they should be.

Keep that picture in mind, and let's look at forgiveness.

AND FORGIVE US OUR DEBTS :
EMOTIONAL : ANGER

Remember yesterday when you got mad at someone and your anger completely took over your joy, and you walked where you shouldn't have walked? You trespassed. You didn't walk in the joy or the patience that could have been part of your daily bread. It was most likely available for you, but… you walked right past it.

A prime example of an emotional trespass…

Consider a time when you "lost your patience" and got angry. That is forsaking a gift that God has plenty of for you personally. You didn't reflect to someone else the way God deals with you… patiently. You blew up and threw up all over them, and it was most likely on someone you care for.

Now it's time for you to ask for forgiveness.

Instead of saying forgive "us" our trespasses, try "forgive ME of MY trespasses." Specifically, think through the range of emotions. A way to do this is to take the nine fruits of the Spirit, and consider what their antithesis or counter-opposite might be.

Think through the range of emotions, a few things may pop up here and there, reminding you… "oh yeah, I did this, or I did that." This is not to heap on guilt, but it's to unearth stuff that may be buried, sometimes just under the surface… rocks that you want to get rid of.

"Forgive me when I walked in anger when I could have walked in the peace and patience You provide".

AND FORGIVE US OUR DEBTS
EMOTIONAL : ANGER
::: Section Reflection :::

Anything you'd like to write down that you
know you need to ask for forgiveness.

_____

_____

_____

_____

_____

_____

_____

_____

_____

_____

_____

_____

_____

_____

_____

_____

_____

_____

AND FORGIVE US OUR DEBTS :
EMOTIONAL : STRESS

This is a huge one. "Really? Stress? A trespass? A debt?"
Remember the verse we read in John? Jesus says,
"Peace I leave with you; My peace I give you."

If God loves us, and God can give us peace… then why aren't we
walking in it? What is it that we are trying to do without Him? What is
leading the train that is pulling us? You? What has led to stress in your life?

Could it be you are not walking where you should be?
Or that you are walking where you shouldn't be? This
emotional trespass plays havoc with you physically! High blood
pressure, heart issues and more are a physical result of an
emotional trespass most likely caused by a lack of spiritual fruit.

A friend of mine went temporarily blind because of
stress. He had an Ocular Migraine! Some kind of massive
headache that affected his eyesight—while he was driving!
He was also dealing with high blood pressure due to stress and diet.
He spent the night in the hospital two separate times thinking
he was having a heart attack, but that turned out to be stress related.

Lately this same friend has been on a new track of
listening to God whispering to him, "I got you." And it's leading him
down new paths of life he never thought he'd be walking in.

When God whispers to you, "I got it," trust Him, and rest
peacefully knowing that He has you!

We so much want to be in control. I wrestle with it all the time.

Is it more freeing and a reliever of stress to ask God His thoughts,
His plans, His ideas you should walk in, and then to obey and do it?

Or, to make up your mind on your own and ask God to bless you along the way, and then have to bail you out when you are at the end of your rope? Thankfully… He does both, and is patient with us. But which way is better and produces the fruit of walking in His will? Stress is the opposite of peace.

"Forgive me, of my trespasses, my emotional trespasses, when I've been stressed ~ when You tell me not to be anxious about anything… sorry for freaking out, taking matters into my own hands, and not trusting You."

AND FORGIVE US OUR DEBTS
EMOTIONAL : STRESS
::: Section Reflection :::

Anything you'd like to write down about stress, anxiety, not trusting God?

_____

_____

_____

_____

_____

_____

_____

_____

_____

_____

_____

_____

_____

_____

_____

_____

AND FORGIVE US OUR DEBTS :
EMOTIONAL : GENTLENESS

For a long time I've had an emotional issue with "harshness" which would be the opposite of "gentleness." If God was as harsh to me as I've been to others, He would have physically and verbally smacked me down many, many times. I struggle to this day... in not answering back my wife in a way that is gentle. It's actually more effective to be gentle than to be a jerk and speaking harshly. Hopefully I'm growing in this area!

Proverbs 15:1 reads, "A gentle answer turns away wrath, but a harsh word stirs up anger."

"Give me the gentleness I need today to do Your will."

And just a reminder as we are headed into the final stages of this book. The goal here is to lay out an idea for us to add to the ways we pray. If you're at all like me and struggle with prayer, hopefully you're getting ideas of how to pray. Keys and concepts, that will change with your days and seasons of life.

I hope you hear several examples that drive home the overall point so that by the end you can go and try it. What is... How to... To Become (where it becomes a part of who you become in Him).

AND FORGIVE US OUR DEBTS :
PHYSICAL

When have you physically walked where you shouldn't have? Let's toss out a couple ideas that might help jog our memories. How about eating? Or drinking? A sin in and of itself? No.

But if you eat deep fried hamburger buns every day, all day, and are so physically out of shape and killing yourself from the inside out, that you are taking away from the activities that a healthier you would be doing, you're affecting yourself emotionally and making yourself unavailable for others spiritually.

Too many times you'll see people who say they are following God, and they are so physically out of shape that if God asked them to climb a mountain and help a person in need… they'd have to say, "send someone else Lord, I'm not physically fit enough for that."

Are we all supposed to be able to run a marathon? I surely hope not! But, how are we physically walking where we should or should not be?

Some other elements of Physical trespasses:

Financially. Have you physically spent where you shouldn't have? And the opposite… have you not given your finances to where you should have given them? Physical trespasses.

Lodging. Have you "bought more than you can afford?" Have you not taken care of what you've been given?

Physical trespasses. Think through that which is physical. In your life… and ask God to forgive you of any physical trespasses that you may have been walking in. *Forgive me of my physical trespasses.*

AND FORGIVE US OUR DEBTS : PHYSICAL
::: *Section Reflection* :::

Anything you'd like to jot down regarding physical trespasses?

_____

_____

_____

_____

_____

_____

_____

_____

_____

_____

_____

AND FORGIVE US OUR DEBTS :
SPIRITUAL

Thank God for His grace! But let's look at where we have spiritually trespassed.

When is the last time you didn't just toss back a spiritual Big Mac and check church off your list of things to do on a weekend?

Your spiritual trespasses cause emotional fruit to die a premature death. And when you end up with an emotionally stunted life, you end up with a physically dead life too.

You are a vessel to carry an emotional, physical and spiritual message to someone. First and foremost, love. If you spiritually trespass you are not only harming yourself, but you are keeping someone else from what God would give them through you!

Examine your spiritual trespasses. And Stop! You have something someone is in need of... don't cut yourself out of the process by just "phoning in" your spiritual growth and walk with God. Or by handing that responsibility over to someone else to do for you. Just like someone can't go and exercise at the gym for you, you and I need to take responsibility for our personal, daily walk with God.

He has more for you... and more He wants to do through you!

"Forgive me for my spiritual trespasses, not taking your Word, or what Your Spirit was whispering to my heart, seriously. Forgive me for not being in Your word and waiting until I drag myself into church to get a little nugget of spiritual input."

He has so much more for us. Repent (stop doing) your spiritual trespass. It will yield emotional fruit!

Forgive us our debts. Forgive me for being spiritually lazy. And for the damage I've caused others because of it.

This may sound strong, but it's good and sound, and we need to press in and keep going… in part 7 we now turn towards forgiving others.

AND FORGIVE US OUR DEBTS : SPIRITUAL
::: *Section Reflection* :::

What spiritual trespasses would you like to stop doing?

_____

_____

_____

_____

_____

_____

_____

_____

_____

_____

AS WE FORGIVE OUR DEBTORS

Matthew 6:14-15 says:
"For if you forgive men when they sin against you, your
heavenly Father will also forgive you. But if you do not
forgive men their sins, your Father will not forgive your sins."

So… remember all the stuff we just prayed through. All the "forgive me when I…" If we can't or won't do He can't/won't forgive us!

Forgiveness runs deep. And sometimes it's hard to
come by. Sometimes hurts seem too deep to forgive.

Forgiveness many times sets the forgiver more free than the one
being forgiven. You may be saying, "I will never forgive him or her of that."
You know, you may be doing more damage to yourself than you are to
the person who you haven't forgiven. To forgive someone of a tragedy
they perpetrated on you or a family member does not mean the act was
ok, or that you aren't still hurt emotionally, spiritually or physically. But
it can mean that you turn that person over to God's hand of justice,
judgment, and wrath. Saying, "Thy Kingdom come and Thy will be done,"
in that person's life… which might include God's judgment and wrath,
now, or later. So forgive, forgive, forgive. Set yourself free and forgive.

Hear this story:
It was Thursday, July 28, 2011 around 10:30 in the morning.
My Pastor Brian Hardin, his wife Jill, and I are following Reverend
Lambert into a church deep within the 1,000 hills of Rwanda.

Seated in front of us are both victims and perpetrators of the
infamous Rwandan genocide.
We were introduced to one young man who began to tell us how
he had killed almost an entire family. Mother, father, children… but
he missed one. She was at the time 15 years old and managed to hide
in the sorghum fields.

She's now 32 years old and smiles beautifully when called upon.
He puts his arm around her and says, "I was the one... I killed her family."
She begins to share... "we were neighbors, our families
knew each other." We ask her, "how could you forgive this man?"
She answers, "how can I not forgive him, if I am going to follow
Jesus Christ?" Still to this day she lives with a friend.
Her family, land, live-stock... gone. Still she has a glimmer of hope.

We then asked the man, "how could you forgive yourself for
doing this?"

He smiles and says, "in prison they came and told us about the
apostle Paul, the man who held the coats as Steven was being stoned
to death." And "we were told of Jesus who said as He died, 'Father
forgive the ones who are killing me' and we accepted this forgiveness."

That is 1 of millions of stories in the 100-day genocide of Rwanda.
A country that is a living, walking, breathing example of forgiveness.

When we returned back to the US, one of the main thoughts we had
was... if they can forgive, let go, and move forward together... why, how
can I justify holding onto the things that I find hard to forgive in others?

When you pray through The Lord's Prayer and you come through
the lines, "As we forgive those who trespass against us," you are speaking a
key to life... but if this key was so important... why wasn't it placed first?

If we can't be forgiven, if we don't forgive... why wouldn't
that be on the top of the list instead of toward the bottom?

I think it's because God is so good to us, so loving and understanding
of us, that unless we worship Him for who He is, we can't see
others how He sees them. As we see and say how great He is, we ask

for His reign and His will to permeate every aspect of our
lives. We then realize what our 'daily bread' is and where its availability
comes from. Then we look at ourselves and see how we've blown it
spiritually, physically and emotionally… Only then do we get to
a place to see others in the light of His big, big grace, and
forgiveness begins to flow a bit more freely from us to others, and from
that… personal freedom comes.

Father I forgive those who have tresspassed against me… It's not
easy. Help me to follow your example of forgiving others, as Jesus
did on the cross, saying "forgive them".

AS WE FORGIVE OUR DEBTORS
::: *Section Reflection* :::

It may not be easy… but who/what do you need to forgive?

_____

_____

_____

_____

_____

_____

_____

_____

_____

_____

_____

_____

_____

_____

_____

_____

_____

_____

_____

AS WE FORGIVE OUR DEBTORS :
EMOTIONAL

I believe that if you've made it this far, you can more easily
identify the thought pattern/heart process of this Ancient Future prayer.

Someone asked, "What do you mean, "future prayer?"
The first thought is, as I type this out it's 2011AD, meaning anno
domini, referring to dates after the death of Jesus. Making this prayer
Jesus gave us more than 2,000 years old, or... ancient. Future is
today and anything past the moment you are in right NOW. Which
by the way just passed. So the future that you have... is based on now
and how you live, pray, trust, and obey with immediate effect.

With THAT in mind, how does the often-quoted verse
Jeremiah 29:11 fit with this Ancient Future Prayer?

"For I know the plans I have for you," declares the LORD, "plans to
prosper you and not to harm you, plans to give you hope and a future."

What is future but now? How is the future anything other than
now... and how we choose to wield or yield our life? It is, this day our
daily bread, which is... what we need today to do His will now.

We do have a hope for the future. And as we yield our now to His
will, and then trust, we will step daily into the future hoped for in Him!

Looking back at forgiving emotional trespasses, how can we
forgive the trespasses of someone who has emotionally sinned against
us? A couple of examples of emotional sin against you might be:

When someone should have been walking in
patience, and they emotionally blew up at you.

When someone should have or could have been
walking in the emotion of love toward you, but because you did or

didn't do something, they did not respond to you with love.

Because someone wasn't walking in peace, they were stressed out and had a heart attack, and you lost a person in your life that could have had an impact.

Who do you need to forgive?

Think through a list of emotions; you can use the fruit of the Spirit as a baseline again: but as you think through each fruit, like kindness, think of how or if someone may have acted in an unkind way and it somehow affected you.

"I forgive those who trespass against me emotionally—especially as I think about this particular person who exhibited or walked in the opposite of the fruit of the Spirit, and it somehow affected me or one of my family members."

AS WE FORGIVE OUR DEBTORS : EMOTIONAL
::: *Section Reflection* :::

It may not be easy... but who/what do you need to forgive?

_____

_____

_____

_____

_____

_____

_____

_____

_____

_____

AS WE FORGIVE OUR DEBTORS :
PHYSICAL

Who has physically trespassed against you? And how? When you consider the various things in your life, that are physical… and you extend the thought process to your family, it can get pretty big. Here's an example: When someone does or does not do something in the physical realm (ie. financially, lodging, transportation, food, etc. *Physical) which somehow has an impact on you or a family member, those things need to be thought about, considered and forgiven. If someone does a faulty job on a car and your loved one is hurt or killed, forgiveness needs to flow. At some point, forgiveness needs to flow.

A great example is Nelson Mandela. He had many opportunities and rights to hate and hang on to bitterness, especially against whites in South Africa. But one of his key attributes that led to global recognition was due to his focus of reconciliation.

Here's another aspect to consider. God gives us what we need when we need it. The young lady in Rwanda who forgave the man for killing her family makes me stop and ponder… and I'd have to say, I don't see how I could forgive in that situation. If God gives us the fortitude to forgive in the scene we are set in… I pray I never need that depth of forgiveness tried or tested in my life, or those that I love.

Remember Jesus on the cross, saying to the Father, "forgive them."

I don't know what you've gone through. But for your freedom. Forgive. To jog my mind, it helps me to think of what "fits" in the physical realm ~ and the more things or areas/sections of the physical, the more I find I need to forgive. Think as you walk or kneel and pray, what areas 'make up,' the physical realm of us humans? Other examples of physical trespasses (anything that has a manifestation in the physical, for example):

Money
Transportation
Lodging
Medical
And so on.

A physical trespass could be someone
overcharging you for something, or taking advantage of you financially.

Medical—Here's an interesting thought (in my opinion):
A farmer in Idaho puts a chemical in his crops that's approved
today but years from now it's realized, "Oops, that chemical is
linked to cancer patients." Your kid had been eating the farmer's
veggies for years, and now at 10 years old your son has a tumor.

Who do you get mad at? God? The farmer? The government?
Your boss for not paying you enough to buy outrageously priced organic
foods? Yourself for not being more careful for what you fed your child?

Who do you need to forgive today of physical trespasses?
How deep do you need to go?
Do you need to forgive them to their faces?
Do you need to forgive them in prayer to God,
and that's enough? At least it's a good start.

"I forgive those who have trespassed against me physically, like…"

AS WE FORGIVE OUR DEBTORS : PHYSICAL
::: *Section Reflection* :::

A couple of lines, just in case you would like to write
something specefic down about someone who has
physically trespassed against you or a family member.

_____

_____

_____

_____

_____

_____

_____

_____

_____

AS WE FORGIVE OUR DEBTORS :
SPIRITUALLY

I don't want to "slam" pastors. I know there are many, many good ones out there. However several I've known, and many who've made headlines, have had affairs against their spouses, stolen money, or in some way or another gone the obvious opposite way than they should have. Many times a spiritual trespass can be less obvious like when we walk in a prideful self-confidence and self-esteem and venture down a path asking God to follow us and bless it. As opposed to asking God for wisdom, direction and insight and following the Holy Spirit, no matter how 'crazy,' it may seem in our culture.

This is not a rant session against pastors. Or "spiritual leaders." But... we have some serious issues in many pulpits. This is not God's doing. Don't let the "spiritual trespasses" of another turn you from God. But rather, toward God.

Forgive him. "As we forgive those who spiritually trespass against us." This is not for just clergy, for co-workers, friends and family, but clergy as well.

Do you know that you don't need to know a person for them to "trespass against you"? God uses people, sometimes whom we don't know, to give us "spiritually what we need today to do His will."

Example: I walk into the coffee shop, get settled in and notice the dude next to me is reading a book; I notice the title and ask him about it. He gives me rave reviews', I go buy the book, and it spiritually enriches me. That may be a pretty lame example, but... the point is, if you are obeying, not trespassing, walking where you should be walking, you may be a benefit, or a blessing to people you don't even know. And the converse is true, too.

Someone may be studying a certain portion of scripture that I'm not studying, and what they were being taught was exactly what I needed for what I was going through or about to go through. But because of their emotional blow up with their spouse they were so upset when I bumped into them, it wasn't shared, and I lost out… I didn't even know they were "carrying something for me" and didn't know I lost out on anything from them… however, they spiritually trespassed and it affected me! Can God get it to me another way? Absolutely. He supplies us everything we need to do His will, and we as people who serve Him can participate… or not. However, I do believe we miss out on something others have for us, because of their sin, trespass, so… try to make sure there's a clean slate… forgive those who trespass.

If a person were "on target" spiritually and dropped something into your life that was effective and "just what you needed," wouldn't you want to thank them? Should you also thank God?

I know this can get/sound a little funky and convoluted, but give it a try when you pray. Ask God to forgive you of your spiritual trespasses and forgive those who spiritually trespass against you.

One day I was walking through our neighborhood and praying, and I thought something like, "If it wasn't for Adam bringing sin into the world in the first place, I wouldn't be struggling with x, y and z…"

Have you ever forgiven Adam? Just a thought. *Onward.*

AS WE FORGIVE OUR DEBTORS : SPIRITUALLY
::: *Section Reflection* :::

Any thoughts about forgiving others who trespass against you spiritually?

_____

_____

_____

_____

_____

_____

_____

_____

_____

_____

_____

_____

_____

_____

AND LEAD US NOT INTO TEMPTATION

You're with your best friend out having a nice dinner together, and you're catching up on life. She tells you that things are well at home and with the kids. You wrap up dinner, and it's time for dessert. First, you're simply asked by the waiter, "Did you save any room for dessert?" You know full well that your best friend is struggling with her weight and is also diabetic. You know that if you ask the waiter to bring the dessert tray over so you "can just take a look," it's not going to go well… but, you do it anyway! The waiter brings over a silver platter with the most gorgeous pies, cakes, and cookies on it, and your friend says, "No, I can't, but you go ahead."

So you order the Decadent Death by Chocolate five-layer fudge cake, and a refill on your diet coke. They actually have a ceremony when they bring out the dish, accompanied by dancers, flame swallowers, and for some reason, a Capuchin monkey (with a little hat). The dish lands in front of you, and you begin to dive in, chocolate is flying, monkeys are screeching and your friend is now crying in her bowl of salad greens!

You may have heard it said… "if doughnuts are your downfall, stay away from the Krispy Kreme!"

You love your children. You would do anything for them. You want them to do well in life, and you want them to succeed. But you tempt them to step into a busy street where they could "learn a lesson," as the cars zip quickly by? Really?!

Would a loving, heavenly Father, who wants the best for us, NEED TO BE REMINDED EVERY DAY: "By the way, I know you are very busy, taking care of more important things than me, but if you could… today… please don't take me by the hand and lead me right down into the path that You already know is going to be temping for me"…?!

Our Father who is in Heaven LOVES us! It is the furthest thing from His character, to take us by the hand and walk us straight into temptations that would cause us to fall apart!

It is audacious when you think about it. God has no pleasure in walking us into areas that tempt us away from Him and His best for us.

So why is it in there? The ancient prayer from Jesus says this: "Lead us not into temptation."

I believe that it is there to remind us of the exact opposite characteristics of God.

Who tempts us? If it's truly a temptation to do what we don't want to do, or should not be led into, then temptation comes from one of three places:

The flesh, the enemy or others.

Romans Chapter 8 verse 7 says: "The mind governed by the flesh is hostile to God; it does not submit to God's law, nor can it do so." 1 Peter 5:8 says: "Be alert and of sober mind. Your enemy the devil prowls around like a roaring lion looking for someone to devour."

Jesus said in Luke 22:46: "'Why are you sleeping?' he asked them. 'Get up and pray so that you will not fall into temptation.'"

And 1 Timothy 6:9 reads: "Those who want to get rich fall into temptation and a trap and into many foolish and harmful desires that plunge people into ruin and destruction."

So again, why is "lead us not into temptation" in Jesus' ancient prayer, in the way that it is in there? We are praying to God and it says, "lead me not into temptation." It doesn't say, "Help others who tempt me to keep a safe distance..."

Or does it?

Take a quick look at James 1: 13-14 (NIV): "When tempted, no one should say, 'God is tempting me.' For God cannot be
tempted by evil, nor does he tempt anyone; but each person is tempted
when they are dragged away by their own evil desire and enticed."

I believe that it is written just like Jesus said it, to remind us daily
that it is audacious to consider that God's character would lead
us into temptation.

I think the only other way to look at it is that, we are actually
asking God not to lead us into temptation. Which would sound
something like this... "God please don't take me by the hand today and lead
me right into the middle of a situation where I would be pushed, challenged
and tempted to divorce my wife." It's just so counter to His character.

Psalm 23:3 reads: "He leads me in the paths
of righteousness For His name's sake."

When I get to this section sometimes I like to pray,
"Lead me not into temptation, but lead me in the paths of
righteousness—right, good paths that will ultimately bring YOU the glory."

And not me the glory. If I were to do it myself, then
I provided—I would get the glory and the pride of being the provider.

When I take the lead and ask God to bless my pursuits, I
ultimately get the glory, and then give a "thank You for our food" shout-
out to God—even though I can't see how it is that He provided for me,
because it was all by the work of my hand. When we follow, we don't
lead. He leads and gets the glory.

When we spend time with God, and He tells us something, we should believe what He says. Trust Him when you can't see how it's going to work out. If you believe you are obeying and you end up against an impassable wall… He will make a way! Peace, I give to you. It may go against everything in you, everything you were raised with, and your entire culture that surrounds you… but will you trust Him?

You can get the glory, or He can. If you get the glory…you have your reward. Let's move into how this links to being delivered from the evil one.

BUT DELIVER ME FROM THE EVIL ONE

In John 10:10, Jesus says: "The thief does not come except to steal, and to kill, and to destroy. I have come that they may have life, and that they may have it more abundantly."

If we look at the obvious scriptures on what is at enmity with God, and with the plans He has for our lives, we will quickly see that it is:

Our flesh (thanks to Adam, but we forgive you, just as the second Adam [Jesus] came to forgive us);

Others (Ps. 1:1 says, "Happy is the man who does not follow the advice of the wicked or take the path of sinners");

Satan the evil one, the thief. If we are going to take God at His word, the Bible, then there is a heaven and there is a hell. There are angels and there are demons; there is a Holy Spirit who came to be our comforter, and there is a devil that seeks to take us out at our weak spots. The enemy of our souls does not come at us where we are strong. He comes at us in areas that he believes we can be tempted in, to fall away from our 'first Love.'

But in Christ!? We are offered life and freedom abundantly. Whom the Son sets free is really free. I've come that they might have life. In super abundance!

What does that mean? It does not mean that you've hit the Jesus jackpot and you'll get a free jet plane and eat nothing but steak and lobster on silver platters in your castle here on earth…

I think I see some of what it means in John 10:9, when Jesus says: "I am the door. If anyone enters by Me, he will be saved, and will go in and out and find pasture."

Find pasture?! We are "His sheep." What do sheep need? Pasture, food, peace, provision for the day, to do whatever the shepherd wants them to do.

So it begins to sound like this:

"Lead me not into temptation, lead me in the right paths that bring You glory and deliver me from the evil one, keep evil far from me and my dwelling, far from my family. And WHY do I think I can ask You to do this?! Because YOU have the Power to do this!"

The enemy comes to kill, to steal and to destroy. Which are three distinct things, and we have three distinct areas of our lives... body, soul and spirit.

John 10:10 reads: "The thief comes only to steal and kill and destroy; I have come that they may have life, and have it to the full."

The definition of kill is to cause something living to die. The definition of steal is take something unlawfully. The definition of destroy is demolish.

The enemy comes to kill us emotionally. To cause something emotionally living to die. Total annihilation emotionally, to take you out at the knees, in areas like love, patience, kindness.

Where have you seen in your life, and in the lives of those around you, where the enemy has come to cause something that was emotionally alive to die?

The enemy comes to steal from us emotionally. Stealing is different than killing. If stealing is to take something unlawfully, what lawfully is ours? Christ came to give you peace!

The enemy comes to destroy us emotionally. To destroy is different than to kill or to steal. When I see my 7-year -old son destroy a lego structure that he has built, he smashes it and it doesn't look at all like it did. He doesn't steal it. He de- molishes it. Dismantles it without any concern. It's smashed!

How does the enemy of your soul take a baseball bat and smash what's being or was built in you or someone you know... emotionally?

Physically... how does the enemy come to **destroy physically**? When you consider that which is physical around us, people, things, the world we live in. In what ways has destruction been rampant? The enemy comes to kill... steal... and destroy. But Christ came to give life, restoration, reconciliation.

Physical theft. In what ways have you been physically stolen from?

The enemy comes to kill spiritually. To cause something spiritually alive to die. Deception. Mistrust. Lack of belief. Fallen spiritual leaders. And on and on.

What are some ways the enemy skillfully brings about death spiri- tually in the lives of people? If true, life-giving spiritual growth and daily relationship with God is the desire of God's heart for you and I, what are some ways **that** gets snuffed out and in many cases, completely killed?

The enemy comes to **steal** from us **spiritually**. To spiritually take something unlawfully from us. Picking away somtimes, little by little. Other times, total grand theft.

What are some ways you've seen the enemy come in and spiritually begin to rob, steal from you or others?

"Deliver me from the evil one, who comes to find ways
to spiritually destroy and rip down, or demolish in my life, what
could be being built up to bring life to me and others."

When we run by "deliver me from the evil one" and flippantly
just think, "God, don't let the devil get me," we could be skipping by
a significant aspect that needs consideration. But because we start
running short on time, and we need to "get moving into our day," (and
I'm talking about what I do all too many times) we may be missing
something that is staring us right in the face and needs to be dealt with.

For me lately, and I see it as I'm typing this out, the enemy has
been trying to steal from me spiritually. In areas of doubt and fear.

So, take time in this area, as you pray, "deliver me from the evil one."
To look at ways the enemy comes, to kill, steal and destroy. And how that
can look in the three distinct areas of spiritual, physical, and emotional.
Then we need to realize it's God that can do this!
He has the ability to save, deliver and provide!

Which takes us back to worship, and seeing and
understanding the characteristics of God in our final section.

What I, (and you) need to remember is that this book is designed
to be a conversation starter. I look at some of these sections
and think, "man, that's short." And think that it could use more explanation,
examples, or at least more words! Then I remember the goal of this
work is not to tell eloquently written stories, but to offer concepts
to get the point across, with an attempt to offer ways to enhance your
time in connecting with your Creator.

So with that in mind… let's move on.

FOR YOURS IS THE <u>KINGDOM</u> AND THE
POWER AND THE GLORY FOREVER.
AMEN.

When I think of the Kingdom, and those who teach on and reach for the Kingdom, my heart goes to a dear friend Hein van Wyk, a Namibian living in South Africa. You can read about his ministry at www.hopeforafrica.co.za.

When I asked Hein to give me some of his thoughts on "the Kingdom," his reply was extensive and beautiful. I've included a little here… if you want more, he'd be glad to give it to you.

Hein's first reply was:
E. Stanley Jones, the missionary statesman to India said this:
"The Kingdom is God's total answer to man's total needs."

Jones went on to say:
"Seeing the Kingdom gives a focal point to our lives, families and ministries. It gives mission to the Church-a task to fulfill. It gives us our first priority and our final goal. It gives meaning to history, and excitement for the future. It gives us a grid through which we can view all the realities of life."

Hein then gave this Simple Definition of the Kingdom:
"The Kingdom of God is any realm where Christ the King rules."
"The Kingdom of God is the place where the will of God is done."

It doesn't appear around the world that "God's kingdom," is established. It really looks like whoever is politically in control, or whoever has the most money, or the most oil, it's really their world, and it's really their "kingdom," to pretty much do what they want with. When you look at the news, when you look at television and movies, who do we see "running things?" To me, it seems like the strongest, the healthiest, the richest humans win.
All this Bible talk about the last being first, and being a servant, seems totally opposite to the world we live in.

Yeah, well I guess because it is!

It's totally opposite. It's totally upside down. That's why we must remind ourselves at least daily that His is the kingdom. He is very, very patient. It may not look like it... but His is the Kingdom. He can do whatever He wants, when He wants, with whom He wants. His...is...the Kingdom. Don't let His patience fool you into thinking He is absent, asleep or powerless. He exemplifies patience, and He exemplifies love.

You may find it hard to believe, but God knows your every single, solitary thought, and exactly how many hairs are on that head of yours.

Recently, God taught me a lesson. Things weren't going the way I wanted them to go in a few areas of my life, and my thoughts and prayers under my breath sounded something like, "Where are You?" and "Do You really love me?" And on and on.

My teenage son had two issues I addressed with him. One had to do with things at school that needed to be handled better, and the other was with cleaning up his room. With my general complaining during this time with the Lord, my son took note over several days that I was stressed out, not happy, and easily aggravated. Then when I came down on him about these couple of items, in a "not-so-sweet way," his response was, "It doesn't seem like you love me." It made me even more mad, and it also broke my heart, because it was the precise and exact opposite of what was going on in my heart. I do what I do because I love him. I work hard, and try in all aspects to show and share with him how much I love him, and only want the best, the absolute best for him.

God said to me, "That's how you make me feel when you doubt me and my love for you." And that "all I do, I do actually for your best interests—you just need to trust Me."

His really, truly is the Kingdom. The way He wants you to go is best for you. But… the road is narrow. So pay attention, and follow the Leader.

FOR YOURS IS THE **KINGDOM** AND THE POWER AND THE GLORY FOREVER. AMEN
::: *Section Reflection* :::

Write down any thoughts or reflections on "Yours is the Kingdom".

_____

_____

_____

_____

_____

_____

_____

_____

_____

_____

_____

_____

_____

_____

_____

FOR YOURS IS THE KINGDOM AND THE
<u>POWER</u> AND THE GLORY FOREVER.
AMEN.

In the book of John chapter 20 Jesus says, "Because you have seen me, you have believed; blessed are those who have not seen and yet have believed."

How many times have you given up on God because you didn't "see" Him come through?

His is the power. He has the power to do it! To walk and work with you to execute His will, which is far better than anything you could have thought up yourself. If we would just walk in the paths He has for us on a daily basis.

Isaiah 26:3 reads: "You will keep him in perfect peace, whose mind is stayed on You, because he trusts in You."

As I write this I am hearing the news of Japan's 8.9 earthquake and subsequent tsunami, with special attention being focused on the potential meltdown of the Fukushima Daiichi Nuclear Facility. It has pushed all turmoil in the Middle East, Libya, and Egypt to secondary status in the news. Not to mention those starving around the world, AIDS and malaria, drug and human trafficking. On and on it goes, while we in America struggle to pay house mortgages and make car payments.

So what is it? What is the bottom line? I recently asked some friends, "In the light of everything we know, what's the most important thing we can be doing?"

I heard different answers like, "pray," and "tell people about Jesus." Some would say spend more time with your loved ones, or do those things you've put off all your life.

I'm not meaning to let you down, but what this book is not... is advice from a guy who thinks he knows the answers. What should we be doing? My answer at this point is "obedience." Obeying what we are individually supposed to be doing. Your "doing His will" will look different than mine. Not in the items that are "set in stone," like… don't kill, steal or stab people in the back. But things like, what should I be specifically doing with my life? God has the power to do it… when our aim is to do His will.

It's going to look totally different for you than it is for me, but if we are not "obeying," what are we doing? Following the cultural streams, doing what our family and education say we are to be doing?

We are in a state of emergency, and most of us are asleep at the wheel. We are more interested in the latest blockbuster movie, how our favorite team is doing, how much cash we need to be making, and the hottie that just strolled by. So, should we all stop playing Angry Birds and kill our flat screens? I think the point is… what God is asking YOU to do is going to look different from what He asks of anyone else. So, you seeking Him today, asking Him today, and listening for Him today is key. Hear… and obey.

This approach is not, "If you give me this God, I'll promise to follow You the rest of my life…" This posture says, "I'm following You today!" My plans, my purposes I lay down, to hear You and to follow and obey. Your plan is the best, and You have the power to execute.

Execute what? Whatever it is that is Your will for me.

Matthew 24:12, 13 says: "Because of the increase of wickedness, the love of most will grow cold, but the one who stands firm to the end will be saved."

In Matthew 19: 25, 26 Jesus is talking about rich people, and the disciples asked: "Who then can be saved?" Jesus looked at them and said, "With man this is impossible, but with God all things are possible."

His is the Power! Trust Him.

My friend pastor John McGuire gave me a word picture, an image of "what faith is like." He said something like this, "Faith is less like a river and more like a lake, and we are in a row boat. When you're in a rowboat you face backward from your destination. God is calling us in a particular direction, but many times we do not see it until it's behind us. And we see a reflection of His will, His story, His glory in the wake we leave behind."

I like that image. I also know that if it's a beautiful, peaceful lake and our stressful, erratic strokes are what we leave behind, stressing out over job, money, fighting our lusts, etc. then we will not leave behind a wake that has smooth, consistent, beautiful, faith-filled strokes that lead us to His destination for our lives, within the Peace that He offers amidst any storms.

His is the kingdom… His is the power.

FOR YOURS IS THE KINGDOM AND THE
POWER AND THE GLORY FOREVER. AMEN
::: *Section Reflection* :::

How does this section relate to you? What are your thoughts?

_____

_____

_____

_____

_____

_____

_____

_____

_____

FOR YOURS IS THE KINGDOM AND THE
POWER AND THE <u>GLORY</u> FOREVER. AMEN.

In Psalm 29 you'll see:

"Ascribe to the LORD, you heavenly beings,
ascribe to the LORD glory and strength.
Ascribe to the LORD the glory due His name;
worship the LORD in the splendor of His holiness." And
The LORD sits enthroned over the flood;
the LORD is enthroned as King forever.
The LORD gives strength to His people;
the LORD blesses His people with peace."

In Matthew 5:16 you'll read: "Let your light so shine before men, that they may see your good works and glorify your Father in heaven."

1 Corinthians 10:31 urges: "Therefore, whether you eat or drink, or whatever you do, do all to the glory of God."

We have smashed down our interaction with God to a prayer before meals! He is so interested— not even interested, but desiring to lead and guide us to walk in "His will being done."

When I get through walking, especially in a setting where I can just focus on praying, and not be too distracted by traffic or whatever, and I pray through this Ancient Future prayer model (combining the Lord's prayer and the whole person, spiritual, physical and emotional), I get to this, "Thine be the Glory" part and it's just, "Wow!" There is no other way. No other way I would want it, no other way He would want it… no better way! If I do whatever I do out of my strength and my brilliance, people would say, wow, that Mike is something else."

But may I… may we… walk in the right perspective that it is
God who directs and sustains us, when we seek and obey Him.
And thankfully, He is so gracious and patient with us when we
walk in our pride and fear, and try to do it ourselves.

I offer these thoughts to you as a hope—that for you, you
will begin to interact with Your Father on a deeper daily
basis and that it begins to affect your life and those around you.

Let the thoughts of this book again, be like the jangling of
keys, 1,000 thoughts that make up a concept. A concept that
never gets stale. A prayer that works for anyone, everywhere.

When Jesus was asked by His disciples to teach us how to pray,
He didn't fumble for words, or say make it up as you go along. He
gave us a life, and life abundantly. So grab the keys, test the examples.
You've seen the, "what is," the "how to," now go… **become** a person
of rich daily prayer and relationship with your Creator. He loves you.

Walk with Him.

And Jesus answered and said:

OUR FATHER IN HEAVEN,
HALLOWED BE YOUR NAME.
YOUR KINGDOM COME.
YOUR WILL BE DONE
ON EARTH AS IT IS IN HEAVEN.
GIVE US THIS DAY OUR DAILY BREAD.
AND FORGIVE US OUR DEBTS,
AS WE FORGIVE OUR DEBTORS.
AND DO NOT LEAD US INTO TEMPTATION,
BUT DELIVER US FROM THE EVIL ONE.
FOR YOURS IS THE KINGDOM AND THE
POWER AND THE GLORY FOREVER. AMEN.

I sit down to work on the final edits of this book. It's been a pretty bad weekend, in that I've felt super sick. From Friday through now, Monday morning… fever, coughing, hurts when I swallow. No exercise, hardly any prayer. Finally feeling better, I get cleaned up, head out the door. Land at 5 Points Starbucks in friendly Franklin, TN and thing after thing goes downhill! More distractions than regular, electronic technical issues, and so on. I am nowhere near at a place where I should be emotionally to wrap this up… So God nudges me, and says something like, um, take a walk. Eventually, I get around to it and take a fairly short walk… that is why I think this was important to add. Practice helps! Now after practicing the model prayer, through the lenses of the three-layered man… those times when I don't have (or take) the time to pray and say everything that needs to be said, and hear everything that needs to be heard… the richness of the Lord's Prayer pours through the cracks and the rich and deep meanings of each part stick to my guts and to my mind, and to my heart. This now doesn't make me want to 'cut it short,' but shows me God's patience with me… once again. And moves me to the next time, when I grab ahold of the time and spend it walking, hearing, telling, learning, gaining wisdom and direction with my loving heavenly Father… and I can't wait.

There are several items in the Christian walk that are tantamount, and most of us feel guilty that we don't do them enough… things like praying, telling other people about Jesus, and reading the Bible.

I felt years and years of guilt in not being in the Word enough. I would hear different viewpoints from the pulpit like, "If you're not reading four chapters a day, you're not reading the Bible enough."

Others would lean on "quiet time." They'd say, "If you don't have a half hour or hour of "quiet time" per day, you're blowing it."

So I always felt this underlying sense of guilt that I wasn't doing enough. My times of prayer were so sporadic and many times non-existent, until this pattern of the Lord's Prayer and the three-layered man became ingrained in how I pray. Now, I love it! Sometimes it's still a challenge to get up and go walk and pray, but every time I do, it actually shapes my journey, and feeds my spirit.

The same is true for the Bible. In the past I would read a little here and there, never getting the grand scope. Always little nibbles from proverbs or Psalms, and in the Gospels until I discovered the Daily Audio Bible. It's been about five years now, and I've been downloading and listening to the Podcast on a fairly regular basis (almost daily).

Even then, another wave of guilt would hit me as I'd listen to the Bible: "You're nothing but a fat American downloading and listening to scripture." And, "If you were really spiritual, you would get up at four in the morning and by candlelight read, and read, and take notes, and use multiple highlighters, and have study tool helps… Then, you'd really be doing well, and studying God's Word correctly."

Well… that just hasn't been me. But, I can say this: Daily, or at least very regular exposure to large chunks of Bible on a consistent basis, has transformed my life. I am not here to heap guilt on you. But I am extending to you what I know is something that can be done by busy people, and it will transform your life.

Don't wait until January 1 to "turn over a new leaf" and decide you're going to read the Bible through in a year. Start now. Download today's reading of the Daily Audio Bible, read by Brian Hardin, and you, along with tens of thousands of us, will listen and journey through the Bible together.

* This is a one-two punch, a winning combination: praying through the Lord's Prayer, keeping in mind that we are distinctly three-layered people; and the Daily Audio Bible daily reading, (or listening). You will be taking spiritual vitamins that will affect your life and those you influence.

Psalm 12:6 reads: "The words of the Lord are pure words: as silver tried in a furnace of earth, purified seven times."

Here is the prayer challenge. Take this example of *An Ancient Future Prayer*...and try it.

Pray through the Lord's Prayer as the structure, the bones. And layer in the aspects of the three-layered man for three weeks. Don't be discouraged if you skip a day; don't be discouraged if you run out of time and can only get half way through. Stick with it as a type, as a model, and try it for twenty-one days.

Here's what I can guarantee: If you pray from your heart and believe, and you trust God that He knows what He is doing and where He would like to take you, you will look back on the wake of your life and see a difference. You will see and say things like, "Oh! That's why I felt in my heart to do that thing that didn't make sense at the time... But now I look back and see why You did that, and it was because You love me, and it was for Your glory!"

If this book has meant something to you, give one as a gift. Find someone that you think might like it, and just take a risk; who knows what keys you may be unlocking in your life and in theirs?

And accept the challenge of a "one-two punch," latch onto the Daily Audio Bible on your phone or computer and dive head first into the Bible like never before.

Psalm 119, verse 105 reads: "Your word is a lamp to my feet, and a light on my path."

And 2 Timothy 2:15: "Be diligent to present yourself approved to God, a worker who does not need to be ashamed, rightly dividing the word of truth."

If we are not in the Word, we cannot know the Word. And if we don't know the Word, how can we pray according to the Word? I love you and appreciate you going on this journey with me.

To God be the glory. Yours, Mike

WWW.ANANCIENTFUTUREPRAYER.COM
WWW.DAILYAUDIOBIBLE.COM